THE BETRAYAL
OF THE SLUMS

BY
THE RT. HON.
CHRISTOPHER ADDISON, M.D., M.P.
FIRST MINISTER OF HEALTH

HERBERT JENKINS LIMITED
3 YORK STREET ST. JAMES'S
LONDON S.W.1 ◈ ◈ MCMXXII

A
HERBERT
JENKINS
BOOK

WYMAN & SONS LTD., PRINTERS, LONDON, READING AND FAKENHAM.

CONTENTS

THE BETRAYAL
OF THE SLUMS

CHAPTER I

THE BETRAYAL

IT seems but yesterday that the people of this country with one accord came forward to oppose aggression. Our word had been pledged to defend another nation against an unprovoked attack, and our honour was at stake. From rich homes and from poor, from mansions and from tenements people came and freely offered their labour or their lives. In that time of trial it was seen more clearly than ever before how dependent we are upon one another, how, in its turn, this class or that comes to fill a vital part in the defence or maintenance of our organised national life.

Almost at once certain weaknesses and neglects in the training, equipment, organisation and physical capacity of the people became apparent, often with a tragical revelation. It was realised with a poignant acuteness that the drab, unsavoury and unhealthy conditions under which so many of our people have to spend their lives, were not only a great drawback to our working efficiency, but a real danger to the State.

At that time men of all sections, realising these conditions, declared that they would engage themselves not only to secure emancipation from the burdens and perils of war, but to unite in a sustained endeavour to improve the conditions of life of those millions of our fellow-countrymen who inhabit dilapidated cottages or wretched tenements in mean streets, and who are destined to struggle continually against conditions which produce gravely disabling effects and constitute altogether a menacing weakness to our whole society.

Responsible leaders of the Government were forward and eloquent in promising that the effort should be made and should be persevered with. There can be no doubt that many a young man who died for his country derived some comfort from the conviction that in the time to come there was a brighter hope for those whom he loved at home and that they had some prospect of escape from squalor and of the attainment for themselves and their children of a better opportunity in life.

The pledges in question were of a very definite character, and were often repeated. They were embodied in a precise form in the Housing and Town Planning Act of 1919, and the records of the proceedings thereon bear witness to the fact that one of the difficulties of the Minister in charge of the Bill was to resist proposals which would have made the task exceed the limits of any possible form of execution. The intention of the Government to persevere in this effort was very clearly stated to the people in the manifesto of the Prime Minister and Mr. Bonar Law when their support was solicited at the General Election of 1918.

The Prime Minister at one time declared that in this matter " the interests of public health and humanity are at stake."

The issues involved were clearly expressed by Mr. Bonar Law, who said : " If we did not make every effort to improve the condition of the people, we should have a sullen, discontented, and perhaps angry nation, which would be fatal in the last degree to trade, industry and credit." The national intention also was forcibly stated by Lord Long— who knew, as well as any man could know, that thereby we were committing ourselves to a work of restoration that must occupy many years of continuous effort—when he said : " It would be a black crime, indeed, if we were to sit still and do nothing by way of preparation to ensure that when these men came back they should be provided with homes with as little delay as possible. To let them come back from the horrible water-logged trenches to something little better than a pig-sty here would indeed be criminal on the part of ourselves, and would be a negation of all that had been said during the war."

Finally, His Majesty the King, on April 11th, 1919, evoked universal acclamation when he expressed the policy of the Government in these carefully considered words :—

" I am informed that the immediate need of working class houses for England and Wales alone is estimated at approximately 500,000. To meet this need the same untiring energy and enthusiasm will be needed as that which enabled the country to meet the demand for munitions of war. It is not too much to say that an adequate solution of the housing question is the foundation of all social progress. If this country is to be the country which we desire to see it become, a great offensive must be undertaken against disease and crime, and the first point at which the attack must be delivered is the unhealthy, ugly, overcrowded house in the mean street, which we all of us know too well."

Many people gave loyal and ungrudging help to the Government in this matter because they believed that no distraction would turn them from a resolute endeavour to fulfil the noble and solemn promises given to those whose loyalty and sacrifice had been abundantly revealed, and who had no place worthy the name of a home for themselves and their families.

It was therefore a matter for grave concern when it was decided, in July, 1921, to set aside these engagements and to restrict assistance in the building of houses to a number substantially identical with that arranged for at the end of the month of March and, worse still, to ignore the obligations which the State had assumed under the law passed in the year 1919, whereby assistance would be afforded in the replacement or improvement of insanitary dwellings for some years to come, and to substitute a grant in respect of all the unsatisfactory houses in Great Britain which, as will appear, is of so trifling a character that it will not suffice even to make good the amount of deterioration that is progressively occurring.

This decision involved not only an alteration in the method of rendering assistance in the improvement of housing conditions, but a definite reversal of policy. This was denied at the time, but it has become progressively manifest during the past year. Assistance from the State was required in this matter because the insanitary and overcrowded conditions of multitudes of the people's dwellings had arisen whilst we were content that private enterprise alone, or substantially alone, should be expected to meet the necessities of the case.

On March 9th, 1922, the Minister of Health, in reply to a question in the House of Commons, expressed the hope " that future State intervention in any form will not be required, and that the building industry will return to its pre-war economic basis."

It would no doubt be an inestimable advantage if private persons once more were able to build houses for working people at such a cost that the rent paid would be sufficient to provide a proper and adequate return upon the capital invested. But the fact that this course alone had hitherto failed either to mitigate the evils of slum life or to prevent their increase, was the primary cause of State assistance being required.

That the present policy involves a complete reversal of that previously declared and embodied in legislative form was further explained by the Minister of Health a short time after the reply in Parliament just referred to.

In an interview with a representative of the *Daily News* newspaper on March 27th, the Minister stated explicitly that " we must try to get the country back to the old economic system," and, in further reply to questions relating to the difficulties of young married people starting family life under the present overcrowded conditions, he is reported to have suggested that " the newly married should be so happy that they can enjoy living even in one room," and further to have said : " But isn't the demand of the newly married for a separate house a comparatively modern development ? In China and the East generally, I understand they continue to live under the parental roof quite contentedly."

It has, I understand, been contended that these remarks were intended to be humorous in some way, but, in principle, they are in complete accord with the statements made in Parliament. The tragic condition under which so many of our fellow countrymen have to live is scarcely a subject for humour, but in any case the pledges given to the people were given seriously and were so understood, and the standards of hope that were set before them bore no relation to those accepted by Eastern people.

An examination of this decision will show that it bears no adequate relation to the needs of the people.

In the last completed year of national expenditure and in the third year after a victory of unprecedented completeness, we were confronted with the position that the tax-payers of the United Kingdom were called upon to contribute, if the sum were distributed equally for every man, woman and child of the population, a sum of 87/3 per head for the maintenance of war services, whilst the burden it was proposed that they should bear for the replacement or improvement of poor homes was to be limited to a charge of 1½d. per head. These figures also of the cost of war services for the year 1921–22, do not take account of all the payments of that class. The additional expenditure, for example, in Mesopotamia and Palestine involved a further taxation of 11/2½ for each member of our population at home.

There is in these things an inequality of effort in the interests of our people at home

B

which is dishonourable and gravely unwise. If a small portion only of what might be saved from this expenditure were devoted to the redemption of slums it would provide a contribution sufficient to pay for the work that could practically be executed during each year. Moreover, this disparity of sacrifice and this disregard of obligations destroy the confidence of those who suffer, and is inimical to ordered progress and to peaceful development.

CHAPTER II

A CLEAR understanding of the case necessitates some review of its attendant circumstances as well as of those associated with the Government's decision to abandon our national effort to deal with it.

For years past thinking and patriotic people of all parties have been seriously disquieted by the fact that in England and Wales alone there are nearly a million dwelling places—so-called homes—which consist of not more than two rooms. People are compelled to live in them, because no other habitations are available. In these places, as well as in vast numbers of others which contain more than two rooms, the processes of deterioration are necessarily constant and rapid. The great majority of them are lacking in many of the simplest amenities, and whilst great numbers by repair or reconstruction could be made fit to live in, it is not disputed that there are at least 200,000 of them which are so bereft of ordinary conveniences, are of so poor a structure and so insanitary, that they are beyond amends, and ought to be demolished. These wretched homes are to be found in every town and village in the land.

In Scotland, the conditions, as revealed in the unanimous findings of the Royal Commission, are, if possible, worse. Nearly half the people of that country have houses that consist of not more than two rooms. Many of them are no better than hovels, and a great proportion are condemned as altogether unfit for human habitation.

Homes of this kind are a perpetual hindrance throughout life to the people who have to live in them. They allow no privacy, afford little or no quiet or rest, even for the child, they give no opportunity for the mind and provide a continual poison for the body. The physical consequences are disastrous to the inhabitants and involve costly burdens on the rest of the community.

From the year 1911 onwards, the building of new houses was less than it previously was. So much so, that for four years previous to the year 1915, in the county of London for example, more working-class rooms were demolished than were provided by new building. During the war there was almost a complete cessation both of new building and of repair, so that by the end of it the conditions had become worse, because the normal wear and tear had not been made good for a number of years. The shortage had become so acute that, coupled with the demand which the war had brought for a better standard of living, public opinion was wholeheartedly in support of a great national effort being made to meet the deficiencies.

In the latter half of the year 1917, and again in March, 1918, specific proposals, worked out by those thoroughly acquainted with the practical difficulties involved, were submitted by the Ministry of Reconstruction, who earnestly advocated that definite preparatory steps should be taken in preparing the necessary organisation, in the acquisition of sites, in the preparation and sanctioning of plans and in kindred matters, and pointed out that otherwise great and unavoidable delays must be met with after the conclusion of the war. The papers and memoranda available bear testimony to the fact that, notwithstanding these repeated and urgent representations, no practical action whatever was taken, and consequently amid the stress of demobilisation and resettlement we were compelled to spend many months making good these neglects.

At the same time, the Ministry presented a scheme of finance, based upon the proposals of Lord Salisbury's Committee, which it recommended on the ground that, after a term of years, the responsibility for any excessive cost would fall upon those who incurred it. This was set aside in favour of the proposal that the State should bear all the loss beyond the proceeds of a penny rate. This latter, whilst simpler and possibly more expeditious in its working, possessed the serious defect of containing no substantial incentive to economy on the part of the local authorities concerned.

During the year 1918 also a number of reliable and experienced people under the Chairmanship of Sir James Carmichael worked out with immense care a scheme for promoting the expeditious and economical provision of building materials throughout the country. Their proposals were based upon an examination of the capacities of the different districts to produce material and of what would be required to stimulate output as quickly and as economically as possible. The general conception underlying their scheme was that, in the absence of the steps being taken that they had worked out in association with the industries concerned, any extensive plan of purchase would lead to an unnecessary inflation of prices. These proposals were somewhat brusquely set aside, and the twelve months' patient labour of the experienced people Sir James Carmichael had called to his aid was wasted. On the contrary it was directed that a large sum of money should be provided wherewith the Ministry of Munitions should make purchases of building material. It cannot be doubted that this decision in conjunction with the competition prevailing during the years 1919 and 1920 contributed to serious and avoidable increases of cost.

In January, 1919, as President of the Local Government Board, the present writer circulated a memorandum, pointing out with complete frankness how unfortunate the position was and how disabling the absence of the needful preparatory work might prove to be.

During the year 1919, although the necessary personnel, both centrally and locally, was not available for many months, the pressure to make haste was very great indeed, and continued substantially throughout the year 1920. The clamour, indeed, even with that section of the Press which has lately vehemently condemned the whole endeavour, was so great that it served to exaggerate the increase of prices that the demand itself otherwise made inevitable. There were many occasions indeed on which the Prime Minister brought great pressure to bear for more rapid progress to be made, notwithstanding that he was fully informed of the increasing cost and of the grave difficulties that it occasioned.

These difficulties arose partly from the neglect of preparatory work, but much more from the fact that an industry, greatly depleted of men, found itself confronted with an unprecedented accumulation of delayed repair work and with those vast demands for new building of all kinds which characterised the apparently prosperous times of the year 1919 and of the early months of the year 1920. Whilst only a small percentage of the men in the building trade were actually employed at that time upon house-building, there was an altogether reckless competition both for men and for materials in connection with contracts for industrial and other building which had been entered into without any definite price having been fixed and which, added to the pressure to make progress with housing, resulted in very alarming increases of prices.

In the autumn of 1919 the draft of a Bill designed to enable us to check the causes of these unwarrantable increases in prices was submitted to the Cabinet. These proposals were not accepted in any effective form, although they were founded on experience gained in kindred matters during the war in respect of which substantial success had been obtained. With the incidence of bad trade, however, and the cessation of much competitive building, prices began to decline, and the reductions obtained during the six months ending March 31st,

1921, were even greater than those secured during the following six months, although many ill-informed statements to the contrary obtained a wide publicity.

Coincident with this decline of an artificial prosperity and in the presence of serious discords at home and abroad, there ensued a sudden and violent reaction. Those who before had been loudest in their protests at the insufficient rapidity of our progress now became the foremost champions in the demand that the housing and slum reclamation projects should be abandoned. It is perhaps inevitable in agitations of this character that the point of attack should be some domestic concern and one with which all the people are familiar. It was so in this case, and services designed to improve the health and housing conditions of the people were at once sought out for denunciation. The just proportion of things is only slowly emerging, and the Report of Sir Eric Geddes's Committee is a noteworthy contribution to public enlightenment. It is, however, a fact that there were branches of national expenditure in which vast economies could be made that came in for little mention and that in those, grouped as war services, our expenditure amounted to as many hundreds of millions as there were tens devoted to all the purposes of health and housing put together.

It will always be a reproach to the Government that instead of informing the people of the real proportions of these things they sought to appease an uninstructed clamour by a hasty capitulation in respect of those services which were designed to improve the lot of the poor and of the unfortunate.

It would be unfair to attribute to the Prime Minister a special degree of responsibility for this lamentable decision if the facts of the case did not abundantly warrant it. The recital of them unfortunately necessitates personal references.

With a view to limiting our commitments to build houses at the high prices then prevailing, whilst at the same time completely honouring the obligations we had entered into with local authorities and keeping the industry employed, it was agreed on March 11th, 1921, after considerable inter-departmental discussion with Mr. Chamberlain, then Chancellor of the Exchequer, that for the present the matter should be left on the basis prescribed by him in a letter to me of March 9th. The agreement in this letter was that I should ration localities on the basis of 250,000 houses, including public utility society schemes, on the understanding that before June, 1922, the matter should be reviewed in the light of costs and of the results up to date, seeing that up to that time the local authorities would have plenty of work to do in carrying out the building thus allotted to them. There was no alteration suggested in respect of the programme for slum restoration work.

Before this arrangement had been announced, at the commencement of the great coal strike and under circumstances which are not material to the present purpose, my work as Minister of Health came to an end, as, at the repeated request of the Prime Minister, I accepted the office of Minister without Portfolio. For some reason with which I was not made acquainted, the arrangement with the Chancellor of the Exchequer was never acted upon. The agitation to which reference has been made was at that time being very actively conducted, and it gained strength in consequence of certain bye-elections adverse to the Government. Towards the end of June, in response to directions which were given without discrimination to curtail expenditure, the Minister of Health circulated a Memorandum in which he pointed out that so far as housing expenditure was concerned no further limitation could be devised beyond stopping the schemes at the point of existing contracts. At the same time he pointed out that a large sum was still required in connection with slum clearances and restoration, and that proposals which would have either of these effects could not be defended so far as the needs of the people were concerned.

On Saturday, July 2nd, I received, marked " for information," the findings of a Finance Committee presided over by the Prime Minister, which had decided to arrest the scheme. I at once challenged the findings of this body, and in the discussion that subsequently ensued received substantial and influential support. So much so that the subject was referred to a specially appointed

Committee. This body met on Tuesday, July 12th, and on Wednesday, the 13th. At the latter meeting, notwithstanding that an important part of the work before us was the consideration of alternative proposals which it had been agreed I should bring forward, the Committee was informed by certain of its members that they had been instructed that morning by the Prime Minister that the findings of the Finance Committee must still be adhered to. In this way deliberations on the merits of the case were brought at an end. I declined to accept an autocratic ruling of this kind on so grave an issue of domestic policy, and resigned my office the next day after the announcement of the decision to the House of Commons.

It will be seen, therefore, that the decision was peculiarly that of the Prime Minister. It limited assistance to new building substantially to the number of houses for the building of which arrangements had been made at the beginning of the previous April, and replaced all our legislative and other commitments in respect of the improvement or replacement of insanitary houses by a grant of £200,000 for the whole of Great Britain.

Before examining precisely the effect of this grant upon the restoration of insanitary areas, there are certain effects of the decision taken as a whole that must be dealt with, and an illustration or two should be given of the immediate effect of its incidence.

CHAPTER III

IMMEDIATE RESULTS

IN the autumn of 1921 a special session of Parliament was called to deal with the subject of unemployment. The numbers of the unemployed were not far short of two million persons. For the greater part of the year 1921 the figures generally were near that appalling total, and even during the month of June, 1922, when this is written, the number still exceeds 1,200,000.

During the autumn session of 1921 proposals were submitted to Parliament that involved the expenditure of large sums of public money in aid of the execution of various public works and otherwise. The Prime Minister had declared that it was the intention of the Government that the building trade should be employed up to the limit of its capacity in the housing schemes of Local Authorities. Many people therefore hoped that at all events some of the public money which was to be devoted to the relief of unemployment would be applied to building a certain number of houses where they were urgently wanted beyond the limit fixed by the decision of the previous July.

It was manifest to every one who had considered the case on its merits at all that it was not physically possible to make good the undertaking with regard to the employment of men in house-building unless the limit were raised, because, as the contracts were gradually completed, the men employed thereon were likely to become unemployed. The proposals of the Government, however, provided for no addition to this work; on the contrary, by a sort of perversity that is incomprehensible, the conditions of grant were so drawn as specifically to exclude any of the money being applied to house-building or even to house-repair work, although a large and increasing number of men in the building trade were out of employment.

One would have thought, if additional public money were to be expended in providing useful employment, that at least some of it might have been spent by employing these men either in building or in

c

repairing a certain number of houses. One cannot with advantage employ a carpenter or a bricklayer or a plumber on ordinary road-making, and the amount of employment for men of their craft in most of the public works which have been aided is very limited. The only alternative method adopted was to assist the unemployed men by a system of doles, or through the poor-law, apart from what they might obtain through their trade unions or from other provident agencies.

Notwithstanding the Prime Minister's undertaking, as indeed was inevitable, the number of men employed on housing schemes steadily declined. In replies to Mr. Trevelyn Thomson in the House of Commons, the Minister of Health stated that the number of men employed on the housing schemes of Local Authorities and of public utility societies had declined as follows :—

	Number unemployed
October 1st, 1921	138,334
November 1st, 1921	134,200
December 1st, 1921	125,344
January, 1922	97,271
*February, 1922	91,175

* A subsequent reply shows that by June, 1922, the number had further decreased to 66,651.

In the course of five months, therefore, 47,000 men who had been engaged in housebuilding lost their employment.

During the same period the number of men registered as unemployed in the building trade and eligible to receive monetary assistance through the Labour Exchanges, according to figures supplied by the Minister of Labour, increased as follows :—

October, 1921 .. .. 130,831 were unemployed
February 1st, 1922 .. 176,119 ,, ,,

It cannot, moreover, be contended that weather conditions were responsible for this, since from an analysis of the trades of the men unemployed as supplied by the Minister of Labour on January 10th the figures were as follows :—

Numbers unemployed in the building trade by occupations :

January 10th, 1922.—Carpenters 12,860
Bricklayers.. .. 7,422
Masons 3,578
Slaters and Tilers .. 605
Plasterers 623
Painters 34,377
Plumbers 3,573
Other skilled trades 6,555
Unskilled 100,752

Total unemployed on January 10th, 1922 168,745

It will be observed that the vast majority of the skilled men unemployed were those concerned with interior work, and it is generally accepted that the employment of two skilled men involves the employment of three unskilled.

Since the month of March, 1922, the numbers of houses being built has further declined, and there has now been a full year of the application of this policy. It is certainly a moderate estimate to say that for fifty weeks up to the end of September, 1922, the Government's decision has resulted in the additional unemployment of 25,000 men per week in the building trade alone. The numbers engaged on the preparation and manufacture of the different materials that enter into a house who have correspondingly lost 'work would of course be additional. Let us, however, confine ourselves to this very low estimate of 25,000 men. What have they cost the community in cash payments from the insurance funds, the poor-law, trade union and other funds ? It suffices again to take a low figure, and it is certainly an underestimate to take the cost altogether at 25s. per man per week. At this rate of benefit there has been expended during the fifty weeks a sum exceeding £1,500,000 in the maintenance in idleness of men able and willing to build or repair houses.

At the same time the statements of the Minister of Health indicate that the price of building has so fallen that, including the cost of land, drainage and fencing, a house may now be provided for £500. On this basis the annual loss on such a house at the moderate rental of 8s. per week, with interest and sinking fund charges at 5½ per cent., would be as follows :

	£	s.	d.
Interest and Sinking Fund on £500 at 5½ per cent.	27	10	0
Repairs, maintenance and empties, say	8	5	0
	35	15	0
Less rent at 8s. per week	20	16	0
Net annual loss	14	19	0

If the million and a half paid to the men for doing nothing were treated as a capital sum, even at the same rate of interest, and putting the annual loss on the house at £15, it represents, at the rent of 8s. per week, the provision, without a penny of loss, of some 5,500 houses. It is difficult to understand how any body of rational beings could persevere in a policy of this kind at a time of such serious unemployment.

The process, however, is still going on, and the estimate given is certainly much lower than the total actual cost.

This is one immediate result of the Government's decision. Let us take another equally serious.

The present Rent Restriction Act expires in June, 1923. This Act and its predecessors arose out of the great housing scarcity. It was found that, owing to the supply of houses being much less than the demand, it was no longer possible to leave it to the free play of the market. A great outcry arose in many places because of attempts to exact large increases of rent or to obtain possession by means of the eviction of tenants unable or unwilling to pay what was demanded. Rent strikes and riots took place in consequence, and in some places where attempts were made to evict ex-service men they were of a violent character.

The Government was compelled, if for no more than for the maintenance of public order and security, to adopt an expedient of this kind. In some form or another, whatever Government is in power, the re-imposition of this Act is inevitable until the housing scarcity is appreciably relieved. So far, indeed, did the demand go when the recent amending Act was before Parliament that it was with the greatest possible difficulty that Parliament was restrained from extending it much further still. It is true that, at present, the Act does not apply to newly-built houses, but there can be no possible surety that this exemption will continue, for people will object just as much to unreasonable increases of rent or to eviction from a new and convenient house as in other cases. Economically unsound and damaging in some directions as these Acts certainly are, they must be continued until the shortage of housing accommodation has been so overtaken as not to occasion injustice and hardship when freedom has been restored.

The fact is, however, that we are very far from overtaking even half of that shortage. Before the year 1910, even under the system which accompanied the creation of our slums, there were on the average some 75,000 new houses of the working-class type provided annually to compensate for wear and tear and for new provision. From 1910 onwards until the war there was a substantial reduction in the average rate of new building. During the four and a half years of war there were not more than 50,000 such houses built in the country altogether, so that by the beginning of the year 1919 the arrears of new building, altogether apart from the arrest of slum replacement or restoration, had mounted up to a prodigious figure. The hardship and overcrowding that exist from one end of the country to the other are sufficient evidence of the truth of these statements, apart from the estimation of any gross totals.

In the face, then, of this scarcity, only a small percentage of which has yet been provided for, with the Rent Restriction Act on the Statute Book and its extension inevitable, the special scheme of extra provision has been brought to an end, and it is proposed to look to private enterprise to make up the deficiency.

But what does private enterprise require ? A man who makes it his business to build houses, just as much as another who manufactures pieces of cloth or who builds engines, will continue to carry on his business only so long as he finds it profitable to do so and so long as he possesses a reasonable opportunity of making the best of the products of his enterprise. Notwithstanding the gratifying fall in the costs of building, the cost of building a house, providing the land, doing the drainage, fencing and other necessary work involves a capital expenditure far greater than the average rents obtainable will provide a sufficient return for, even in industrial areas.

In country districts the discrepancy is much greater owing to the standard of rent and of wages having been reduced by the practice of providing cottages at nominal and uneconomical rents. If, however, by a further substantial decline in building costs the building of cottages by private enterprise became a nearer possibility, the Rent Restriction Acts would still be present to the mind of the builder. At any time he might be deprived of his freedom in dealing with the property in which he had invested his money. Human nature and the facts of the case being what they are, it is certain that there will be no sufficient revival of house-building by private enterprise so long as the Rent Restriction Acts continue.

Therefore, at one and the same time the Government prevents the accumulated shortage being made good by State or municipal assistance and, by prolonging the shortage, commits the community to the continued operation of that statute which effectively prevents its being met by private enterprise.

We need refer only to one other general consequence of the effect of this decision before entering upon a closer examination of the problem presented by insanitary and dilapidated houses.

Its effect was immediately paralysing upon all the work that had been undertaken in response to the pledges that had been made. For the first time the authorities, great and small, throughout the country had made an examination of the needs of the people in their district in respect of overcrowding or of dilapidated or insanitary houses, and had set before themselves with remarkable unison a thought-out scheme of improvement which would gradually be carried into execution during the years to come. Their labours were brought to nought ; all their expenditure of time and thought was made to end in disappointment, and patriotic people of all creeds and classes turned away with sorrow from disinterested public service. Impulses and forces of that kind cannot easily be mobilised, and having once been brought together with a worthy purpose before them and having then been dissipated, they cannot be gathered together again for a long time. The loss to the nation of all this goodwill must be well-nigh incalculable, and it is appropriate in closing this chapter to give a brief account of what I saw at that time when taken round by a public authority, to witness, as it were, the funeral of their hopes.

With great courtesy the Mayor and Corporation of the City of Wakefield invited me to visit them. The number of new houses to which they had been limited under the new decision was 200. They required more than four times that number for additional accommodation alone, whilst they were further confronted in the city with no less than 1,100 inhabited houses which were condemned as unfit. Many of the latter were in an area in which the death rate was 27, whilst that for the city as a whole was 15·6. In that same area the death rate from tuberculosis, with all its resulting charges to the ratepayers, was three times as great as in the city as a whole. Tenement after tenement, row after row showed the same squalor and insufficiency of decent accommodation. A soldier who had looked for a home lamented the fact that he was now shut out from the possibility of obtaining one. His family occupied a single room looking out on to the wall of a narrow court. It served for kitchen, scullery, coal cellar, wash-house, living-room and bedroom, and was rented at 7s. per week.

It is to be noted also that there was only one vehicle to be seen in that street, and it was the carriage of the relieving officer.

In the afternoon a neighbouring authority, similarly limited, invited me to inspect some farm buildings at the end of which two families had their abode, and for whom now there was no chance of betterment. In both families the husbands had seen long war service. One tenement provided for a family of four, and the other housed a young couple who had one child. Both men were of good character and with regular employment. The tenements of each were similar— a room below served as living-room and kitchen, and in both cases the diligent wife had made the very best of it, both as to comfort and cleanliness. Up a steep, narrow and rickety stair we found their sleeping-places. There was one room above the kitchen and another, scarcely larger than a good-sized cupboard. The larger family had to use both, but the young soldier at the back had had to abandon the larger room, not because of the falling plaster or the broken and sinking floor-boards, but because there were so many rats with runs in and out of the skirting-boards that they disturbed their sleep. The rats had even invaded the furniture. The human inhabitants had surrendered and taken to the small room because it was somewhat freer from vermin. The little room was freer from the rats, because beneath its floor-boards there was no harbourage for them as it formed a part of the roof of the pig place. It is true that the grunting of the pigs disturbed the family somewhat, but that was less objectionable than the rats.

I thought of Lord Long's moving pledge as to the places that are no better than pigsties, and which he said, truly, that it would be a " black crime " to continue to tolerate.

The man whose family was thus housed was a clean, fresh-faced young Englishman who had served through the war. For four years he had been a prisoner of war in Germany, and after his emancipation this was all he could secure for a home. But the fresh colour in his face was deceptive, for on coming down the stairs from seeing the bedroom, I saw a familiar coloured form on the table that he had received that morning. On reference to it, it transpired that he had been found to be suffering from tuberculosis, and had been summoned to go for sanatorium treatment. One does not wonder at his having contracted tuberculosis. He will cost the State about £2 15s. per week while he is a patient in the sanatorium. The bed that he will occupy has cost the State £180 to provide, apart from the contribution of the local ratepayers. These charges will continue for many months, and if we add to them the cost of the maintenance of the wife and child during that time, and the loss of his work and earnings, it is not difficult to discover that the occupancy of that barn-end will have been a costly business.

The tragedy and the sorrow of such cases as these are not to be concealed from the people. Disappointment may well give way to bitterness, and the economies demanded in these things by the apostles of " Anti-Waste," which were so precipitately conceded, may indeed prove to have been an extravagance. Cases like these, existing as they do in abundance throughout the land, are seeds of bitterness ; the harvest of them may be delayed, but it is continually ripening in sorrow and in sullenness, in disputes and in diminished production, and the garnering of it will be very costly.

CHAPTER IV

WHAT THE PROPOSED GRANT WILL DO

AS a result of the Government's decision, Local Authorities will not receive the assistance to which the Housing Act of 1919 entitled them. Under that Act any losses they might have incurred beyond the proceeds of a penny rate, upon all their housing expenditure, including what they spend upon the replacement or restoration of insanitary houses during five years, would have been made good to them. This is to be replaced by a grant not exceeding £200,000 a year for the whole of Great Britain.

Before examining the application of this proposal it is necessary to refer to certain conditions and limitations that attach to all schemes of restoration work of this kind, whatever may be the form of assistance.

The magnitude of the task acts as a barrier. Apart from the hundreds of thousands of new houses that are required as new accommodation to compensate for overcrowding, it exists sufficiently in the insanitary houses which are to be found in all our towns and villages. A low estimate, as already stated, is that 200,000 of them in England and Wales are so derelict and insanitary that they can only be demolished and an equivalent number of new dwellings provided. Beside these there is a very much greater number that require substantial repair or reconstruction before they can be said to comply with the most modest standard of what a home for a family should contain.

In Scotland 539,000 homes, or more than half the houses in that country, consist of not more than two rooms in all. Apart from overcrowding, the Royal Commission unanimously, found that 57,000 of them were so damp and abominable that they ought to be cleared away.

These houses have gradually come to their present state, and the private owner has often had little or no power over the events which have led to these results. In a great number of cases the houses, either individually or in small groups, are in the hands

D

of people of relatively modest means, and it is certain that in the great bulk of cases the private owner has neither the money nor the credit to carry out the necessary reconstruction and repair work. If he had, he would incur great loss by executing the work at present or prospective prices and rents.

For the most part, private enterprise can only carry out a reconstruction scheme and realise a profit when the greater part of the ground or property is devoted to commercial or industrial uses. When this happens the result aggravates the existing overcrowding.

A Local Authority in the first instance does all it can to secure the execution of the necessary repairs and sanitary improvements by the private owner. When this has been exhausted, it finds itself confronted with a great number of bad houses which either ought to be demolished and replaced by new accommodation, or subjected to such reconstruction or adaptation as the present owner cannot afford and cannot fairly be asked to carry out.

When an area consisting for the most

part of this class of property has to be dealt with, the best and most economical use can be made of it only if the Local Authority acquires it as a whole. This necessitates a considerable commitment in respect of purchase, and the preparation of a scheme or plan of however provisional a kind, for dealing with it as a whole for housing and for other purposes. In other words, unless the transaction is to be unnecessarily wasteful, the Authority must commit itself to an undertaking which will require some years to carry out, and of which the execution is complicated by the fact that reconstruction or replacement must be proceeded with piecemeal if the area is at all considerable, because of the hardship from dishousing that would otherwise be occasioned.

Such property, under the provisions of the Housing Act of 1919, can now be acquired on terms which, it is hoped, will cease to put a premium on slum property, and at the same time be just both to the owners and to the public. Nevertheless, under the most favourable conditions any Local Authority, in committing itself to an improvement scheme, has to accept extensive obligations, and the burdens it will cast upon the ratepayers must be a governing consideration.

It is accordingly recognised, both by Statute and by common consent, that the responsibility for the existence of extensive bad housing in different places is not one that can rest wholly upon the locality itself, since the conditions have resulted both from lack of national policy, and from social or industrial circumstances over which those inhabiting the particular district have had little or no control. Indeed, housing improvement has stood still in poor areas, and will continue to stand still unless outside help is afforded, because the poorer the district and the more dilapidated its houses the less is its credit and its ability therefore to deal with them. In addition to this, the national disabilities which result from bad housing have led all sections of opinion to recognise that national assistance in some form should be afforded.

Unless, therefore, the share of the grant which a Local Authority will receive bears a reasonable relation to the amount of assistance that the task before them requires that they should obtain if the burdens upon their own ratepayers are not to be of a prohibitive kind, no scheme will be undertaken that will be sufficient to produce any substantial amelioration of the present evil conditions. If this does not prove to be the case, then the effect is to deter authorities from preparing effective schemes of improvement. The consequence in such cases inevitably is that matters will go on getting worse, for the amount of deterioration that the present overcrowding is causing, even in property that is not yet classified either as dilapidated or insanitary, is extensive and is accumulating. No inducements that amount to anything more than occasional coats of whitewash are going to accomplish anything in the reclamation of our slums or in the prevention of their extension.

The effect of the grant may best be tested by applying it to cases where the Authority is strong financially and is well equipped with able and experienced municipal executive officers. If it proves to be insufficient in such cases, it will certainly be quite inoperative where the Authority is poor, possibly inexperienced, and saddled with the burdens of an overcrowded and badly-built district.

We will therefore examine it by applying it to the cities of Leeds and Glasgow, relying for a statement of the facts upon two Government publications.

The first case will be found stated in the Second and Final Report upon Unhealthy Areas recently presented to Parliament by the Committee presided over by the Rt. Hon. Neville Chamberlain, M.P., and the second is contained in the unanimous findings of the recent Royal Commission on Housing in Scotland.

In the City of Leeds Mr. Chamberlain's Committee informs us that there are 72,000 houses built back-to-back in close parallel rows, without through ventilation and without any circulation of fresh air being possible.

An examination of these houses shows that 12,000 are fairly substantially built, and have fifteen feet of space between the front of the house and the road. They also have a separate w.c. entered from this space. These are the best houses of the 72,000.

The second group consists of 27,000 houses built in blocks of eight. Between each pair of blocks there are sanitary conveniences for the inhabitants of each of the two groups of eight houses. In order to get to these places the people have to go along the street, as there is no garden or court of any kind attached. These are the second best houses.

The remainder consist of 33,000 houses built back-to-back in long continuous rows, opening directly on to the street, and crammed together at the rate of seventy or eighty to the acre. The sanitary conveniences and the houses themselves are so atrocious that, we are informed, it is difficult to suggest any satisfactory method of dealing with them short of complete clearance.

Now a small part of the grant may be reserved for specially hard cases, but substantially it must be distributed, as all such grants are, on a population basis. The Secretary for Scotland has already told us that the share of Scotland is to be £30,000. On that basis the City of Leeds will receive somewhat less than £4,000.

If we omit the 12,000 of the better houses of the insanitary class, the grant for Leeds in respect of the remaining 60,000 represents a subsidy of one shilling and fourpence per house per annum. If it were confined to the second class, it would represent three shillings per house per annum, and if it were confined to the worst of all and to those only that need demolition and replacement, it would be equivalent to assistance to the extent of half a crown annually for each house. Is it to be expected that the municipality of Leeds will enter upon the acquisition and reconstruction of the 27,000 houses that are worth reconstruction, or of any substantial number of them, entirely apart from the demolition and replacement of the 33,000 that are altogether condemned, with the help derivable from a grant of these dimensions?

On a basis twice as favourable as that existing at present their allowance may suffice to meet the charges falling upon them for the reconstruction of 250 of these houses at the most, leaving not a penny over for any other purpose.

It is a mockery to suggest that the City of Leeds will be induced to undertake its gigantic task or any sensible proportion of it by an offer of that kind.

How would the proposal affect Glasgow? In this city, in the year 1911, there were 32,742 houses consisting of not more than one room, and they accommodated 104,621 people, or more than three persons in each room. At the same time there were 75,536 houses consisting of two rooms, which provided homes for 267,341 people. These two classes of houses together therefore provided dwellings for 470,000 people, or a little more than 62 per cent. of the total population of the city. That percentage was the same ten years previously, and it has certainly not improved since then. A large number of these dwellings, besides being overcrowded, are utterly insanitary and inadequate. It is not a misuse of words to say that in these dwellings the City of Glasgow is presented with a problem of appalling dimensions. Its share of the Scottish grant is estimated to be about £6,000!

Test it where we will, the grant affords no material help and provides no scheme of policy for any place that is handicapped by bad housing conditions. It leaves the burden still upon the inhabitants, and present conditions testify to the evil results of that policy.

In view of the fact, however, that this decision may be maintained it behoves us to look closely into the conditions governing the lives of people under these circumstances and into the results which follow to themselves and to the community.

CHAPTER V

LIFE IN SLUM HOUSES : ITS GENERAL CHARACTER

WHEN we examine the results of living in overcrowded or insanitary houses, we are apt to turn to the mass figures of census returns and of Government Reports. Such figures, however, may give no adequate indication of those underlying realities from which alone we can obtain either a true understanding of the position or guidance for future action.

It will not be needful, therefore, to give many figures.

The census of 1911 revealed that in England and Wales 3,139,472 people were living in 430,000 tenements at the rate of more than two occupants to each room, and that there were 915,182 houses in the country that consisted of not more than two rooms. The recent census has revealed an increase in the population in England and Wales of 1,814,750 people, but the corresponding figure of over-crowding is not yet known. The diminished rate of building since 1911 and the absence of repair work during the war make it certain that the number of people living in over-crowded conditions will be substantially increased. In the City of London in 1911 there were 758,786 people living under such conditions.

According to the recent Report of the Royal Commission, there were 399,876 people in Scotland living in houses of one room only, and 1,881,529 others living in houses of not more than two rooms, so that in effect 2,281,405 people or nearly half the population of Scotland lived in houses of one or two rooms. So far as the condition of these houses is concerned, the Royal Commission says :—

" To our amazement, we found that, if we take overcrowding to mean more than three persons per room, we should, to secure even this moderate standard for Scotland, have to displace some 284,000 of our population. But this is not all. We conclude that at least 50 per cent. of the one-room houses and 15 per cent. of the two-room houses ought to be replaced by new houses. . . . For such gigantic figures our Report submits full justification. On this point the Commission is unanimous."

The foregoing figures, however, are limited by the definition adopted for the term " overcrowded." In England and Wales the standard adopted is that of *more than two* persons for each room and in Scotland of *more than three* persons for each room. Such statistics, moreover, tell us nothing of the vast number both of people and of houses beyond those so overcrowded, in which the conditions are insanitary and in which the inhabitants are not supplied with bare facilities for the ordinary and decent conduct of family life. When these are taken into account, as they must be, and as they were in the returns made to the Ministry of Health in 1919, the numbers of those who have to live under unhealthy conditions is enormously increased. Whatever may be the shocking total, the figures in their very greatness reveal one thing that cannot be challenged. They show that any suggestion that the people concerned are made up of thriftless persons cannot be entertained at all. In the main they are working people who live under these conditions because there is no opportunity for them to live under any other.

It is not the people's fault that their life is spent in unsavoury tenements wherein they and, often enough, two or three other families have to share the same water tap in the yard or on the next landing, as well as a dirty closet which it is nobody's business in particular to keep clean. It is no fault of theirs that the mother of the family has only an ordinary fire-grate in which to cook the meals and that the same room has to serve as wash-house, living-room and bedroom. It is not their fault that there is no possibility morning, noon or night, for any member of the family to have any manner of privacy whatever; that the infant and the little child have to sleep in the room which others have to frequent when they come in for supper and during the evening; that it is not possible for fresh air to get through the tenement because it opens either on to a stuffy landing or is backed by another house; that the boys and girls have to sleep in the same room together ; that even at the time of birth, or in the hour of death, the same unyielding conditions, save for the kindliness of neighbours, similarly circumstanced, govern the whole conduct of their family life.

There is no over-statement in any of this, but it is better to take the facts as they emerge from unchallenged and impartial inquiry.

We have seen that more than half the population of the City of Glasgow live in one or two-roomed houses and make up a population of 471,982 persons—a greater number than is contained altogether in many of our important towns and cities.   Dr. James Burn Russell was for twenty-six years the Medical Officer of Health for that City, and later became the Medical Member of the Local Government Board of Scotland.   He spent his life studying these conditions.   His testimony is beyond question and is worthy of study.*

He wrote as follows :

" Figures are beyond the reach of

---

* " Public Health Administration in Glasgow." Memorial Volume of the Writings of James Burn Russell, B.A., M.D., LL.D., edited by A. K. Chalmers, M.D. Maclehouse & Sons, Glasgow. 1905.

sentiment, and if they are sensational, it is only because of their terrible, undisguised truthfulness. You must not think of the inmates of those small houses as families in the ordinary sense of the term. No less than 14 per cent. of the one-roomed houses and 27 per cent. of the two-roomed contain lodgers — strange men and women mixed up with husbands and wives and children, within the four walls of small rooms. Nor must I permit you, in noting down the average of fully three inmates in each of these one apartment houses, to remain ignorant of the fact that there are thousands of these houses which contain five, six and seven inmates, and hundreds which are inhabited by from eight up even to thirteen.

"I might ask you to imagine yourselves, with all your appetites and passions, your bodily necessities and functions, your feelings of modesty, your sense of propriety, your births, your sicknesses, your deaths, your children—in short, your lives in the whole round of their relationships with the seen and the unseen, suddenly shrivelled and shrunk into such conditions of space. I might ask you, I do ask you, to consider and honestly confess what would be the result to you? But I would fain do more. Generalities are so feeble. Yet how can I speak to you decently of details? Where can I find language in which to clothe the facts of these poor people's lives and yet be tolerable? . . .

" It is obvious that no manner of occupancy will make the one-room house a home in the proper sense of the word. Not that many an isolated man or woman or aged couple may not find in it a wholesome and suitable dwelling-place and enjoy therein the privilege of independence. Even the young couple who have ' married for love ' while yet in the stages of ' working for siller ' may light their first fire on the hearth of the one-room house. These are the anomalies of life, and, under certain conditions, I take no exception to the one-room house in itself, because it undoubtedly meets them ; but, I repeat, a home in the proper sense of the word, a place for the nurture of a family, it can never be . . .

" But," he goes on to say, " let us ask ourselves what life in one room can be,

E

taken at its best. Return to those whose house is one apartment, and consider whether, since the world began, man or angel ever had such a task set before them as this—the creation of the elements of a home, or the conduct of family life within four bare walls. You mistresses of houses, with bedrooms and parlours, dining-rooms and drawing-rooms, kitchens and washing-houses, pantries and sculleries, how could you put one room to the uses of all? You mothers with your cooks and housemaids, your nurses and general servants, how would you in your own persons act all those parts in one room where, too, you must eat and sleep and find your lying-in-room and make your sick-bed? You fathers, with your billiard-rooms, your libraries and parlours, your dinner parties, your evening hours, un-disturbed by washing-days, your children brought to you when they can amuse you, and far removed when they become trouble-some, how long would you continue to be that pattern husband which you are—in one room? You children, with your nurseries and nurses, your toys and your picture books, your space to play in without being trodden upon, your children's parties and your daily airings, your prattle which does not disturb your sick mamma, your special table spread with a special meal, your seclusion from contact with the dead, and, still worse, familiarity with the living, where would you find your innocence and how would you preserve the dew and freshness of your infancy—in one room ? You grown-up sons, with all the resources of your fathers for indoor amusement, with your cricket fields and football club and skating pond, with your own bedroom, with space which makes self-restraint easy and decency natural, how could you wash and dress and sleep and eat, and spend your leisure hours in a house of—one room ? You grown-up daughters, with your bedrooms and your bathrooms, your piano and your drawing-room, your little brothers and sisters to toy with when you have a mind to and send out of the way when you cannot be troubled, your every want supplied without sharing in menial household work, your society regulated and no rude rabble of lodgers to sully the purity of your surroundings, how could you live and preserve ' the white flower of a blameless life '—in one room ? You sick ones, in your hushed seclusion, how would you deport yourselves in the racket and thoughtless noise of your nursery, in the heat and smells of your kitchen, in the steam and disturbance of your washing-house, for you would find all these combined in a house of—one room ? Last of all, when you die, you still have one room to yourself, where in decency you may be washed and dressed, and laid out for burial. If that one room were your house, what a ghastly intrusion you would be. The bed on which you lie is wanted for the accommodation of the living. The table at which your children ought to sit must bear your coffin, and they must keep your unwelcome company. Day and night you lie there until with difficulty those who carry you out thread their tortuous way along the dark lobby and down the narrow stair through a crowd of women and children. You are driven along the busy and unsympathetic streets, lumbering beneath the vehicle which conveys your scanty company to the distant and cheer-less cemetery, where the acid and deadly air of the city in which you lived will still blow over you and prevent even a blade of grass from growing upon your grave."

This is a terrible portrayal, but it is not beyond the sober truth, and it would be possible to multiply quotations from evidence presented to Parliament in official Reports which reveal the character of the family life of people whose unfortunate lot it is to live under these conditions. It will be useful, however, to record an example from the results of an inquiry which was conducted in North-East London shortly before the war, and which on more than one occasion was made effective use of by the Prime Minister in public speeches.

A complete report of domestic conditions was obtained from a considerable number of streets. Many of the houses were not in the condemned class, but for the most part had become inhabited in tenements. As a typical case the records may be quoted of the first ten houses on the same side of a street for which the information was complete and in

which the houses, so far as their structure
went, were in a sound condition, and which
are fairly representative of tens of thousands
of houses which exist throughout the country.
A recent examination of the street reveals no
substantial change. It is described as " a
medium broad street of three-storied houses,
with basements. The basements are always
dark and unfit for habitation. The houses
have fairly large windows and fairly lofty
rooms. The yards at the back are of a good
size, but are shut in by houses at the end."

The accompanying table speaks for itself.

House.	Number of Lettings:	Population:		Total.	Number of W.C.s in the House.	Number of Water Taps in the House.
		Under 18.	Over 18.			
1	6	11	9	20	2	2
2	4	19	8	27	2	2
3	4	18	6	24	2	2
4	6	5	8	13	1	1
5	8	—	10	10	1	2
6	8	21	13	34	2	1
7	5	19	10	29	2	1
8	7	16	13	29	2	1
9	7	22	12	34	2	1
10	4	12	6	18	2	2
Totals	59	143	95	238	18	15

The fact that one water-closet served on the average rather more than three separate lettings, and that the tenants of nearly four separate lettings had to share one water tap for all purposes, gives perhaps a better indication of the way that family life is carried on than any bare figures of over-crowding can do.

It was ascertained beyond question that the population in these streets consisted almost wholly of average working people, regularly employed, who were constant residents. Many of them, indeed, had been born there. They lived there because it was " handy for work," because they could not get other accommodation, because the father and the children liked " to come home for dinner," because they " could not afford railway fares from the suburbs," and because they were near a cheap market, and finally because they " just lived there."

There is no point in multiplying examples, for there are many miles of such tenement streets in London alone. It is better to consider the effect of such surroundings on the people concerned.

CHAPTER VI

LIFE IN SLUM HOUSES : SOME OF ITS RESULTS

OFFICIAL statistics in municipal and other reports prove that life under the conditions described in the previous chapter is accompanied by a high death-rate, and is conducive to the spread of tuberculosis and other diseases. Let us endeavour to get behind these reports and examine the effect on the general vitality and efficiency of the people.

As to the statistics, Dr. Russell told us that 32 per cent. of the children who die in Glasgow before completing their fifth year, come from one-room houses, whilst only 2 per cent. come from houses of five rooms or more. But such figures may be submitted to various corrections affecting the total numbers and ages of those concerned, and Dr. Chalmers, the present Medical Officer of Health, as quoted by the Royal Commission, made allowance for all the different factors affecting age-rates and otherwise, and found that the mortality statistics in the different classes of homes was as follows :—

Death rate per house in

One-roomed houses	..	..	..	20·14
Two-roomed ,, ..	..	..	..	16·83
Three-roomed ,, ..	..	..	..	12·63
Four and more ,, ..	..	..	..	10·32

In Birmingham, Dr. Robertson, the Medical Officer of Health, took two comparable industrial areas within that city, the one with some 33,000 houses on a little less than 2,000 acres, and the other with 30,000 houses on about 3,000 acres. The first area he described as having bad living conditions, and the second as providing fairly good accommodation. The results were obtained from the records of the years 1912 to 1916. In the first area, the general death-rate was 21 ; in the second 12. In the first, the infant death-rate was 171 ; in the second it was 89.

With regard to tuberculosis, an inquiry was made in some London boroughs as to the home conditions of those who came to the dispensaries. In one borough only 86 out of 482 consumptive patients had a bedroom to themselves, whilst nearly all the remainder shared not only a room, but a bed, with some one else. In another case, only 134 cases out of 766 had a bedroom to themselves, and 453 of the remainder shared a bed with one or more members of the family.

These things are impressive enough, but it is only when we apply the conditions to an ordinarily healthy physical life, that we get some understanding of the disablements by which people in overcrowded dwellings are handicapped and are rendered more likely to become a burden upon their friends and fellow citizens.

Take first the case of sleep.

The growth of a child, and the health, both of the child and of the adult, are much dependent upon a sufficiency of sleep. For a number of years, a child spends, or should spend, at least half of its life in bed, and if because of the noise outside or that caused by other occupants of the same room it has insufficient opportunities for quiet sleep, its growth and health are injuriously affected. We are all familiar with the fact that, if at any time we have suffered from a lack of sleep, our ability to do our work, our good temper and general bodily and mental health begin to suffer. But in these narrow homes it is not possible for the children to get sufficient sleep if the ordinary conduct of family life is to be possible for the mother and father and for the older members of the family. If they are within doors during the evening, they cannot but disturb the sleep of the younger ones or make them go to bed later than they ought to do. This consideration, as well as the character of the home itself, often compels the seniors to find their occupation in the streets or elsewhere.

How can they be blamed if they sometimes go to the public-house more than is good for them ? It provides free conversation, as well as shelter and warmth when it is raining and cold. In the presence of these obvious facts it is a little difficult to understand why so many well-meaning people have resisted all attempts to make the public-house a pleasanter place than it is. Apart from them, too, society owes more than it sometimes suspects to the numerous clubs and associations that help to brighten the evenings of the people in these crowded districts.

In homes of this character wherever there is a family, and despite all the ingenuity and expedients that parents may devise to abate its drawbacks, there is an ever-present obstacle from infancy onwards to the children getting a sufficiency of quiet sleep. There is not one of us, more fortunately circumstanced and with young children of our own, who has not passed in the evening along such streets and seen tiny children playing about doorsteps and on the pavement at a time when our own were already in bed. It needs no expert to convince us that plenty of sleep is essential for a child's growth and good nutrition, but these children are handicapped in that way from the beginning as the records of the school medical service will presently reveal.

The case is made worse because of the fact that their chances are usually prejudiced in two other matters almost equally vital to good health : namely, in the quality of the air they have to breathe and in the character of the food they have to eat.

It is plain that the air in our home, of all places, should be as pure as we can get it, because we breathe it for a longer time than any other. The mother of a family spends most of her time within doors. The children spend at least two-thirds of theirs. Even grown-up persons who go to daily work and return in the evening, spend nearly half of their lives at home, if we take the whole year round. When people, for all these hours, are breathing air largely used by others, too crowded in their rooms, and very often in rooms that cannot be ventilated, it is inevitable that they should be injured thereby and become specially prone to the infection of colds, tubercle and other complaints.

We have all experienced at different times the lassitude and ill-effects which arise from a long stay in a stuffy room ; but this is not the occasional, it is the usual condition in multitudes of these homes. Take those 72,000 houses built back-to-back in the city of Leeds, and which, being shut in by a wall at the back, cannot possibly have through ventilation. The only opening in such cases, beside the front window, is the door, which opens, often enough, on to a landing that is stuffy and that is shared by the inhabitants of other tenements in which the air is similarly stagnant. Under these circumstances, it is unavoidable that medical inspection of school children should show that hundreds of thousands of them suffer from various disordered throat conditions ; from chronic catarrh, enlarged tonsils, adenoids and the rest. Great numbers of the children, owing to the spread of the affections from the throat to the ear, become affected with deafness, with all its attendant disadvantages when they come to have to earn a living.

The case of food is equally striking and is equally traceable. A great proportion of the houses now used in tenements in this country were originally designed for single-family occupation, and in most of them the room that was originally the kitchen is the only room in which there is a fire-place on which a woman can cook meals with the usual facility. In the other tenements of the house, the women have to do the best they can with their pots and pans perched on the bars of an ordinary fire-place. Even when this is not the case, there is usually no proper provision for keeping the food fresh and clean, either before it has been cooked or afterwards. Too few of us realise under what continual disadvantage the heroic mothers of millions of our people have to labour in the conduct of their home life. These disabilities, of course, affect the family diet every day. They limit very much the kind of meals that can be cooked, and impose sameness and lack of variety upon their food. One consequence often is that there is an excessive use of ready-cooked foods, pickles, and of other tasty things difficult to digest. Continued through a series of years, diet of this kind is represented by widespread digestive disorders. The proportion of the working classes that suffer from them is very high indeed as the records to which I shall shortly allude bear testimony.

An interesting side-light on this aspect of the question is afforded by the experience gained during the special efforts which were made during the years 1919 and 1920 to combat the high infant mortality. Great endeavour was made to concentrate our efforts both centrally and locally on the improved milk feeding of infants. It is not material here to detail all that was done, but the simple diet of milk that the infant requires afforded an opportunity to secure that in

that section of the child's life the natural
uncooked food should be available in suitable
form if the child's mother was herself unable
to provide it. The results were most gratifying; but what could be done at that stage of
life could be done afterwards if the conditions allowed it. As soon, however, as
infancy is past the child begins to share the
family diet and the drawbacks that have
been pointed out begin to assert themselves
and are manifest in defective growth and
nutrition.

It is not, therefore, a matter of surprise
that of the 2,434,252 children in attendance
in our elementary schools, who were medically
inspected during the year 1920, no fewer than
1,166,784 were found to be suffering from
some physical defect or other. There were
500,000 children who were definitely described
as suffering from malnutrition. The wonder
is that there were not more. Their bodies
had been crippled by an early deficiency of
sleep, by improper feeding, and by a perpetual lack of fresh air.

In later life the same causes were revealed
in the large number of undersized and unfit
recruits that presented themselves at the

recruiting stations during the war. People were shocked. It is easy to forget it now in peace time. But our forgetfulness does not abate the constant and continuing operation of these damaging influences. They continue to produce malnourishment and many of the physical disabilities that limit the person's ability to do good and useful work, and to do it regularly. The industrial loss involved must be prodigious, and to it must be added the increased liability to unemployment pay and to dependence upon public support.

Familiar, however, as many of these things are, it came as a surprise to many, two years ago, to find that the insured population of England and Wales lost fourteen million weeks of work through sickness every year. These were people, be it noted, who had work to do, but who were unable to go to it because they were sick. The loss was so gigantic that no study of its causes could be too careful. A detailed examination, therefore, was made of the sicknesses of insured persons as far as they could be ascertained. Three conclusions emerged from the Report with clear and irresistible dominance, and they

F

deserve to be quoted. They were stated as follows :—

"1. That the conditions which impair the health and even lead to the disablement of men, women and children are not chiefly the conditions which kill them, though they may, in many cases, predispose to mortal disease.

"2. That relatively little of the sickness is attributable directly to infectious disease, and

"3. That a substantial proportion is preventable."

Apart altogether from grave diseases, what were the two conditions that bulked largest amongst those for which the people sought medical aid ? They were respiratory disorders, other than grave disease, and indigestion. In representative cities it appeared that out of every thousand disorders for which insured persons sought advice, no less than 324 were accounted for in these two groups.

There are all sorts of risks and disadvantages to be encountered in adult and working life, but such results are not to be wondered at if we consider the home conditions that have prejudiced the air and the food that has been taken by so many people from childhood onwards. It is reports of this kind that begin to reveal the waste that slum life represents in loss of labour and production. in the cost of medical attendance and of sickness payments.

Parenthetically it may be observed that, at the time this inquiry was being made, a determined attempt was made by an important newspaper to do away even with the meagre records that we have of what the people suffer from. It is strange that political malignity should go so far as to seek to deprive us of a knowledge of the causes that prevent people being able to continue at their work because of sickness.

It would be easy, but it is not necessary, to extend this examination of the physical disablements which are so conspicuously present amongst that section of the people which includes so many that are overcrowded and badly housed. The material is ample, and is plainly set out in the report of almost every independent inquiry that has been conducted on the subject.

It may, however, be profitable, seeing that the national effort to deal with these conditions has been arrested on the ground of economy, to inquire a little more precisely into the costs which are otherwise attendant upon the present state of affairs.

In doing so, also, we must defer for the present the consideration of those other results of life under these circumstances which are not ascertainable in terms of bodily ailments, or in cash payments for the sick. They will, no doubt, be present all the time to the minds of thinking people, but the data are not available whereby we can assess the national loss arising out of the misery and sorrow, the discontent and the bad habits that assail with such advantage the lives of those who have to spend their days in these gloomy and unhealthy places.

CHAPTER VII

LIFE IN SLUM HOUSES: SOME ITEMS OF ITS COST

WE have no means of calculating precisely the loss occasioned by the diminished production and by the loss of earnings which accompany preventable sickness. A substantial proportion of the fourteen million weeks of work lost through sickness annually is clearly associated with sickness that is preventable, and it is markedly prevalent amongst that section of the people whose homes we are considering.

We know what cash payments are made through official agencies to those who are sick, and what is spent in various directions in remedial treatment. There are, however, so many deficiencies in our knowledge of the bill of costs, that at the time when I was Minister of Health I directed Mr. Vivian, the Registrar-General, to try and work them out for a single disease. The disease of tuberculosis was selected for that inquiry, because so much of the cost incurred in its treatment is separately accounted for, the payments made to the sufferers are more readily ascertainable, and the cases are notified and are fairly carefully followed up. It happens also to be a disease that is to a great extent preventable and that is very much connected with bad home conditions.

Mr. Vivian had available the costs of sanatorium and dispensary treatment and other official information. He was also greatly aided by the largest of the Approved Societies, who freely placed all their records at his disposal in order to enable him to ascertain the benefits that were paid to members suffering from tuberculosis and the number of weeks of work that they lost. The results obtained may, quite fairly, be taken to represent a general average for tuberculous cases.

It appeared that tuberculosis represented about one case out of every hundred that came before the Society, and accounted for one out of every fifty-five of the cases that received weekly sickness payments on account of loss of work. Owing to the fact, however, that the duration of the disease is prolonged and that tuberculosis patients received payments on an average for nearly fourteen weeks each, against a general average of five weeks, it emerged that out of every £100 that the Society paid in sickness benefits, those affected with tuberculosis received £5 2s., or a little over one-twentieth part of the whole.

It is not necessary to describe the elaborate calculations which accompanied Mr. Vivian's general application of these conclusions. There were 46,318 deaths from tuberculosis in England and Wales during the year 1919, and allowances had to be made for the ages of those affected, their occupations, earnings, and for many other circumstances, before any final estimate of the loss could be arrived at. His conclusion, however, is represented in the following table from which there is omitted from lack of separate data any estimate of the share of the cost that tuberculosis entails upon our public health services.

TOTAL ANNUAL DIRECT COST OF TUBERCU-
LOSIS TO THE COMMUNITY (ENGLAND
AND WALES) :—

	£
Loss by death of production and services calculated to afford a net annual addition to capital of	9,600,000
Loss by incapacity of production and services estimated at, say	2,350,000
Cost of National Health Insurance cash benefits, say	300,000
Cost to public funds of curative provisions, say	2,000,000
Annual Cost—Total	14,250,000

It is to be observed that, although tuberculosis is a long continuing disease, the payments for sickness benefit made in respect of it were only about one pound out of every twenty pounds that societies paid to their members on account of sickness. The remaining nineteen pounds and the corresponding losses and costs that attach to them have to be accounted for. It is in them that we are confronted by the fact already stated that respiratory and digestive disorders, apart from grave and defined maladies of either of those two classes, account for no less than 324 out of every 1,000 disorders from which insured persons annually seek advice. When we couple together the life conditions which favour the occurrence of these disorders with the conclusion that much of the sickness is preventable, we begin to have some glimmering of the extent of our commercial and industrial losses arising from avoidable sickness. All the evidence available goes to show that the sum, whatever it is, is so large that it might well bear comparison with the greatest items in our national expenditure.

From whatever direction indeed this problem is approached, and when all fair allowances have been made for other causes, the conclusion is irresistible that the cost in physical disability, the loss of work and of working efficiency, the cost of payments for sickness, for treatment, for unemployment, for poor law and other charges arising out of bad housing conditions form a prodigious total.

Some further light upon this is provided by a table of our present annual expenditure on medical services which was supplied by the Ministry of Health. It includes expenditure from rates, from the exchequer and from assigned revenues, together with compulsory individual contributions and the cost of hospitals and of voluntary contributions.

It is as follows :—

	£
Proportion of Poor Law charges spent on Health Services	11,000,000
Cost of Asylums and Mental Diseases ..	2,000,000
Cost of Tuberculosis	1,900,000
Cost of Maternity and Child Welfare ..	1,950,000
Cost of the School Medical Service ..	600,000
Cost of Treatment of Venereal Disease	117,000
Cost of Voluntary Hospitals	7,000,000
Cost of Sickness and Disablement Benefits Payments	8,700,000
Cost of Medical Benefit and Drugs ..	9,100,000
Total	42,367,000

It should be noted that the expenditure on tuberculosis treatment directly is one of the smallest items. In comparison with this charge alone, different municipalities state that their expenditure on the treatment of tuberculosis is more than ten times what they will be entitled to receive from the grant of £200,000 for the improvement of the bad housing; notwithstanding that bad home conditions are admittedly one of the most important predisposing causes of the origin and spread of that disease.

The costs already referred to, however, take no account of what we spend on the unemployment which has its origin in physical unfitness to obtain work or to retain it, nor do they include any of the expenditure upon sickness of benefit and friendly societies and of trade unions, or of the numberless clubs, fresh air funds, country holiday funds, convalescent homes, and other expedients which the charitable public through churches, missions, and all manner of organisations support for the amelioration of the conditions of life in crowded industrial districts.

The tragic and disappointing feature of the decision to limit the amount devoted to the improvement or replacement of bad houses to £200,000 is that, whilst itself accomplishing next to nothing, it has the effect of leading to the abandonment of a policy of restoration and prevention, and commits us to a continuance of a system whereby millions are vainly poured out in dealing with results.

It is not possible to separate out those portions of the charges that are directly attributable to bad housing conditions, but the records from the schools, from the poor law, from the trade unions, from the approved societies, as well as from the public expenditure incurred in these districts where bad housing predominates, show clearly enough that they are responsible for a large proportion of the burden. It must be far within the limit of fair statement to say that in as many tens of millions annually they compare with the hundreds of thousands that the Government now propose to devote to their removal.

CHAPTER VIII

SOME METHODS OF DEALING WITH UNFIT HOUSES

IT would avail nothing if we were to confine ourselves to a statement of existing evils and fail to consider constructive suggestions for dealing with them.

The problem is not more difficult than many others, and could certainly be dealt with at less cost than is involved in some branches of national expenditure which yield little to show for what is spent. The task in any case requires to be undertaken with patience and with resolution, sensibly, and with a willingness to learn as we go on.

The first necessity is to avoid highly coloured and impracticable promises, to recognise and to say frankly that any national attempt, however made, to restore or replace unhealthy houses must occupy a long series of years. The British people is sufficiently endowed with good sense and patience to be satisfied if it sees that the policy is being adhered to and that the work is being steadily carried on throughout the country.

The second necessity is to do everything possible to prevent the development of additional insanitary areas. This is particularly necessary, because, so long as the present acute shortage of accommodation remains, there is a continuous tendency, with the increase of the population and with the demolition or disuse of the more dilapidated of the existing inhabited houses, for people to crowd more and more into houses which at present are in good or fair condition, and thereby accelerate their deterioration. It is important, therefore, to continue unimpaired the powers at present possessed by Local Authorities for the maintenance of good sanitary standards and for the execution of repairs, and to secure their fair and vigilant administration.

The few clearances that had been effected before 1919 revealed that an essential factor in the prevention of the spread of insanitary areas is to secure that the basis for compensation, when an area has become condemned as insanitary, should be such as to make it disadvantageous to the owner that property should be allowed to decline to that condition. The system of compensation on acquisition prior to 1919 was such that sometimes it actually paid to let property deteriorate and thereby hasten the day when compulsory acquisition became necessary in the interests of the public health. This wrong was removed by the Act of 1919. Mr. Neville Chamberlain's Committee, however, recommend certain changes in the system of compensation provided in that Act that may prove to be valuable and necessary, but the principle recommended by that Committee, and embodied in the Act of 1919, should not be departed from. It is thus stated by Mr. Chamberlain's Committee :—

" Where a landlord has allowed his property to fall into a condition which is unfit for human habitation, it is not equitable that he should receive anything by way of compensation for the structure, even though he continue to draw revenue from it by reason of the exceptional shortage of accommodation now prevailing."

Let us hope that no political exigencies will lead to such an alteration of the law as will remove what is at present a real inducement to an owner to prevent the deterioration of his property and that enables a Local Authority to acquire an insanitary area without incurring unjust and excessive burdens.

Another important aid in the prevention of additional insanitary areas arises out of the Town Planning powers, which become obligatory upon the larger Urban Authorities after 1923. It has already been proved that where such work is done sensibly and without too much technicality and detail, it encourages good development.

Any scheme of planning-in-advance, however, is closely linked up with questions of transport. People naturally prefer to live reasonably near their work, and to avoid the time and expense of long daily journeys, so that the more transport is improved and cheapened, the less irksome such journeys become, and the tendency to live in more open surroundings is encouraged. It is accordingly useful to afford every facility for the establishment of factories with adequate transport in open country, and for the provision in the same district of well-planned industrial settlements. In this connection, the provision of better opportunities for credit to well-managed garden city associations, public utility societies and similar bodies is important, for it has now been established that where such bodies, under good management, are free to make the wisest use of a good area of land for housing, industrial, or other purposes, it is possible to develop settlements on these lines without any material charge, if any, falling upon public funds.

As a further aid in preventing a worsening of slum conditions, Mr. Chamberlain's Committee make a valuable suggestion. They say that :

" During the time of acute scarcity, Local Authorities might have power to declare an area congested, and to prevent any further demolition therein, or new building except under licence. This might prevent matters getting worse in some places and would be so much to the good."

The foregoing precautions, if diligently

G

adopted, would certainly assist in delaying the spread of overcrowding and of insanitary conditions, but unless much new accommodation is provided and the bad houses themselves are restored or replaced, these measures alone will in no way provide additional room for the population or suffice to compensate for the inevitable decay of poor dwellings.

The decision to limit the provision of additional new houses to the number substantially agreed upon in April, 1921, must therefore have a desolating effect. Added to the decision to limit the allowance for improving bad housing to £200,000, it bolts the door against relief, for nothing can prevent the spread of overcrowding and of insanitary conditions unless there is a great amount of additional accommodation made available.

This is not the place, however, to deal with that aspect of the case, but rather to consider what can be done with regard to the bad houses themselves, on the assumption that the safeguards and precautions already set out have been adopted.

There is certainly no one specific. All possible means must be used. Some may be more appropriate here, others there, and our minds must be open all the time for better and more economical suggestions.

The first question which arises is : Can we leave the task to private enterprise ?

We cannot expect private enterprise to undertake the improvement of insanitary property, except at a fair profit. It has not done so heretofore because it entails loss, and it is the more difficult for it to do so now when the cost of building is enhanced and when limitations have been imposed on rents by the State itself because of the housing scarcity.

There are properties to be found, even in bad areas, where the houses are kept in a good state of repair, and the best is made of them. In these instances, it is usually a well-to-do owner that is responsible, and one whose property and interests are large enough to make good estate management possible and profitable. In the majority of cases of poor-class houses, however, the houses, through a series of leases and sub-leases, are in the immediate charge of people of relatively small means. Sometimes it is a house-farmer whose sole interest is to do as little as possible to the property and to get as much out of it as possible. If, however, we set this last class aside, it is still true that, even when the disposition is there—and it often is—the cost of putting the houses into a really tenantable condition, when structurally worth it, is often beyond the means of those concerned, and would be unremunerative in any case.

Much minor repair work is done, it is true, by owners of this class of property on their own initiative, or at the request of the local authority, but when all this has been allowed for, there remain such a vast number of houses which are really hopeless, and so many more which can only be rendered fit by considerable reconstruction, that the private owner has neither the money nor the credit to deal with them even if he were disposed. He can, as a rule, only control a few houses out of a great number, and he is thereby continually confronted by the fact that, apart from losing money by his work, he would find himself possessed of houses still much depressed in value by adjoining insanitary property. In practically all cases, where considerable insanitary property has been dealt with privately, it has been for the purpose of demolition, and for the devotion of the greater part of the site to commercial or industrial uses.

The task, clearly, is not one that private enterprise will undertake. Indeed, it does not appear to be seriously questioned anywhere that the great bulk of the necessary practicable improvements in insanitary areas can only be effected by a public authority after it has purchased the property for that purpose, nor is this conclusion seriously affected by making a full allowance for the work of the different, more or less charitable, housing trusts.

How then can a local authority proceed in these matters ?

Whenever a local authority becomes responsible for an improvement scheme in any area, it must purchase the whole or a considerable and appropriate part of it, otherwise it would not be able to make the best use of the ground on well-planned lines either for rehousing or for the leasing of suitable sites for commercial and industrial purposes. In any other case it would have used the ratepayers' money to enhance the value of property which later on it would need to acquire.

A local authority has the power of purchase already where an improvement scheme is contemplated, but Mr. Chamberlain's Committee makes the additional suggestion that, —since reconstruction or demolition with rehousing can only proceed on a few areas at a time and on them piecemeal and by stages—a local authority should be enabled to purchase the property in an insanitary district for the purpose of executing such improvements as may be possible both in management and in conveniences apart from a scheme of general reconstruction.

This additional suggestion of Mr. Chamberlain's Committee appears to be valuable, because it would bring some immediate help to those districts which practical considerations rule out from reconstruction or rebuilding work for the time being.

Apart from the gradual demolition and replacement of worthless houses, there is a large number of unsatisfactory or insanitary houses that could by various schemes of reconstruction be turned into useful and clean dwellings. Many ingenious schemes of this kind, limited to a few houses, have been carried out in different places, and it is manifest that no cut-and-dried rules should be made prescribing what should be done. It is pre-eminently a matter on which local initiative and enterprise, with full knowledge of the character of the local population and of its needs, should receive great freedom and encouragement. But the houses that are worth reconstruction and repair, as distinguished from those that need demolition and replacement on the site or elsewhere, are not usually separately situated. They exist in adjoining streets in the same area or even in the same street with others of a worse kind, and involve considerable commitments with regard to acquisition.

In every case also there is a displacement of the population during reconstruction, although the houses would be dealt with in small groups. In any event the former overcrowding would not be repeated. Nevertheless a very substantial contribution to housing improvement can be obtained by such reconstruction schemes when the state of the property makes it worth while. At the end of such a process, however, we are still left with the great block of worthless and insanitary property that must be demolished and replaced as well as with the overcrowding unprovided for. Any local authority, therefore, in planning this kind of work needs to have these other considerations before them.

The work in any case involves considerable preliminary expense. A scheme of a provisional kind for the area has to be prepared, negotiations have to be entered upon with a large number of owners and other interested parties, many detailed and technical questions affecting compensation and other matters require to be discussed, notices have to be served, and a host of commitments of a diverse kind have to be entered into.

A local authority in undertaking the work also requires to be satisfied that they will be able to carry it through however generous may be the allowance of time that has to be made for the purpose. It is the destruction of this confidence, necessary both for initiation and for execution, that has led authorities from one end of the country to the other to abandon beneficent schemes of house improvement.

No substantial progress will ever be made unless reasonably sufficient national support is absolutely assured throughout to the authorities concerned. There may be some who would question this statement and inquire as to why the burden should be, in part, a national one. It is rather late in the day to ask such a question, but the answer is not far to seek.

In most cases the overcrowding and accompanying conditions have come about through industrial and other changes over which those affected have had no control. There has been no requirement anywhere of planning-in-advance or of provision for transport or for development. Districts have been built up as trade or industry required, and society has taken no intelligent or considered precaution in advance with regard to the home requirements of the people concerned. They have had to make shift as best they could. The responsibility for this lack of foresight rests upon us all and not simply upon the district concerned. A district ought certainly to bear such a proportion of the charges as will involve a real incentive to economical work and management, but it is entitled to help from the community as a whole, for those whose lot is cast in more pleasant places are equally concerned in the causes which have produced these results and in the benefits that will result to society from improvement. It cannot be denied also that the poorer the district and the more burdened it is by insanitary property, the less is its financial ability to deal with it. The estimates also show that to limit the burden in such cases to the local ratepayers would end in nothing being done because the burden was so heavy.

Every consideration of justice is in support of national help being afforded, apart from the fact that in the absence of such national help the enterprise will not be undertaken at all.

Some one, however, may say, " I admit these contentions ; I admit the awful conditions prevailing and their results ; I admit that the grant of £200,000 for the whole country will do little or nothing and is not in accord with the existing law or with our promises of support, but the financial condition of the country compels me to say that we cannot afford to do more."

The argument which has been followed in preceding chapters has been designed to show not only that ought we to do more, but that it would be wasteful folly not to do more. It remains to be shown that we can do more. Before, however, making any suggestions as to the form and extent of that additional and necessary aid, it is proper to examine those questions of national policy which affect the decision to arrest housing enterprises and that blot out the hopes of betterment that our pledges aroused.

CHAPTER IX

FUTURE POLICY AND A PROPOSAL

THE short period of artificial prosperity that followed the conclusion of the war came to an end nearly two years ago, and no one will question now that we are finding ourselves stricken and impoverished through the losses of the war, and that it is not possible by any devices to escape the consequences of its prodigious waste. The restoration of our financial position, therefore, demands frugality both in personal and in national expenditure, and this applies as much to the costs incurred in the work of restoration as to any other. But the waste is not in treasure only. It is even greater in the bereavements, in the sufferings and in physical and social deprivations of the people themselves, and it cannot be good statesmanship to lose sight of it.

If we are to make up for the losses of the war and to bear our added responsibilities, it is necessary to improve the physical, intellectual and industrial capacity of the people. One of the most poignant lessons of the war, indeed, was that there was a great need for increased efficiency. If this is so, then it must be unwise to neglect one of the chief causes of deterioration. Especially must this be the case when it has been proved that the physical disabilities which follow from present conditions entail heavy burdens of costs upon the rate and tax-payers, and provide a constant cause of social discontent.

With regard to the latter it is common knowledge that multitudes of people are continually suffering disappointment in their search for a home. The following letter may be quoted as an example. It was sent by the Town Clerk of a Metropolitan Borough on July 11th, 1922, to a workman resident in the borough who was anxious to obtain better accommodation for his family :

" I have to inform you that there are at present no vacant houses on any of the Council's estates. Your application has been filed with the many others which have been received, and these will be considered in the event of a vacancy occurring on any of the estates or when the houses now being erected are completed. There are at present about 6,000 applications on the file."

In order fully to appreciate the significance of this letter and the hopelessness that it entails for the applicants, we must remember that the accumulated deficiency in new provision that has accompanied the years of the war was preceded by four years in which, according to a report issued by the London County Council, there were 24,602 working-class rooms demolished in the County of London and only 20,851 built. Even before the war, therefore, the pressure in the County of London was becoming greater, and the 6,000 applicants on the waiting list of one borough alone shows how it has become intensified since then.

Every day brings to thousands of people throughout the land the heart sickness that arises from a fruitless search. The letter quoted is only a fair example of those which have to be sent to people all over the country.

The soreness which these things give rise to in the minds of people who have every wish to be quiet and law-abiding citizens is beyond accounting. We are not faced in this matter with the vapourings of reckless agitators, but with the bitterness that arises with sober people whose only desire is to do their work quietly and to have a home for their family.

It is not disputed that the perpetual unrest amongst the mining population which has lately inflicted such grievous losses upon us, is continually being ministered to by the disgraceful conditions under which the miners in many districts have to live.

So long as these things continue any agitator, however reckless and however destructive of social order his doctrines may be, can find material for his support. Discredited to-day, he comes again to-morrow, for these conditions soon furnish him with new disciples.

It is impossible to calculate what we lose by all this or to say how much it has entered into the ill-feelings and the losses that have accompanied the wasteful strikes of the past three years, but it is plainly incumbent upon us, if we can, so to adjust our national policy and expenditure that sufficient means may be made available for dealing with these things.

Nor is it possible to maintain that it cannot be done.

Expenditure to a great extent is governed by policy, and unless we are prepared to accept the necessary modifications of policy nothing can be done. On certain items of expenditure there will be common agreement. Interest on debt must be paid, and the services which are necessary therefor must be maintained. A steady and reliable system of repayment must also be persevered with, although the amount to be repaid each year may be adjusted to the measure of national prosperity and of our ability to repay. Similarly, provision must continue to be made for those who are entitled to assistance from the State by reason of their services during the war and otherwise.

But there are other forms of expenditure that are open to question. The maintenance of them has already involved the sacrifice of a national effort to improve the homes of the people as well as the curtailment of many beneficial social and educational services.

It may conceivably become the case that in the desperate impoverishment that the war has brought even restorative services may have to be curtailed for a time ; and in any event it is necessary always to be seeking out for better and less costly methods of carrying them on. If curtailment were forced upon us, it would be lamentable, because it would prejudice our recovery, but such an unfortunate necessity can in no wise be claimed to have arisen whilst prodigious expenditure is continued on less essential services.

For the sake of greater clearness it may be well to set out a short table showing the contrast between our expenditure on war services and what we devote to those that are now being considered.

During the financial year ending April 1st, 1922, the moneys provided out of the exchequer for these objects, and reckoned per head of the population, were as follows :*

---

* The population of Ireland is not known precisely, but for this purpose the population of the United Kingdom is taken as 47,150,000, that of Great Britain being 42,767,833.

H

Expenditure on War Services, including Mesopotamia and Palestine	Expenditure. £	Taxation per head of Population. £ s. d.
*Housing (Great Britain), including £5,750,000 subsidy to private builders	233,153,000	4 18 5½
Treatment of Tuberculosis (Great Britain)	11,336,724	0 5 3½
Proposed Grant to Redemption of Slums	2,124,000	0 1 0
	200,000	0 0 1½

It may be claimed that substantial reductions have been effected in war expenditure and that the foregoing comparison does not now apply. It is, however, more than a year ago that the decision was

---

* The subsidy to private builders will practically terminate with the present financial year. It is unlikely that the remaining obligations on the housing schemes will equal £10,000,000, as estimated by Sir Eric Geddes' Committee, because this estimate rests on the money having cost 6½ per cent. to provide for interest and sinking fund. Whenever the local authorities are able to borrow for repayment—as indeed, they already are—at a lower rate of interest, each reduction of 1 per cent. will reduce the subsidy by £1,500,000. The report recently issued by the Ministry of Health indicates already that the estimate of £10,000,000 is excessive by at least a million.

taken which is here challenged, and most of the expenditure has been incurred since that time.

Supplementary estimates have also to be reckoned with. Last year they exceeded £100,000,000, of which some £14,990,000 were for the Army and Navy alone. During the short period of the present financial year also Supplementary Estimates have already been presented to the extent of £8,368,126, of which a material part is for Miscellaneous War Services. The Estimates, however, for the present year for War Services including Mesopotamia and Palestine amount to £152,508,000. If we allow for the necessary adjustments of the accounts in respect of the Middle East, which are duplicated, and make a moderate allowance for Supplementary Estimates, we cannot expect that the total charges will be less than £150,000,000 which represents a taxation, excluding the Irish Free State, of £3 8s. 2½d. per head of the population.

What does this figure include? Sir Eric Geddes' Committee, in their review of naval estimates, made no allowance for the economies consequent on the Washington agreement.

If these are excluded from the present naval estimates, it appears that the reductions effected fall short by some £14,000,000 of those recommended by that Committee, who, all the time, made the most generous allowance for the requirements of national and imperial security.

The Army and Air Service Estimates also contain important provisions which are very significant of the present disposition of our policy.

The charges for War and Air Services in Mesopotamia and Arabia, excluding pension charges to British troops, amount to £8,633,000. Similar charges in Egypt are responsible for a further £4,903,000, and in Constantinople for £2,680,050. These three items are therefore responsible for expenditure totalling £16,216,000.

The Colonial Secretary deserves credit for effecting reductions in the expenditure in Mesopotamia and adjoining countries whilst the present policy is maintained, but one has yet to find a responsible soldier who regards this policy as warranted by any reason of military necessity.

It is to be observed also with regard to

Egypt that Sir Eric Geddes' Committee makes this very appropriate comment :

" The only force which was maintained in these areas before the war was one cavalry regiment and five infantry battalions in Egypt, the provision for which, at present-day costs, would not, we are advised, have exceeded £1,450,000." *

The vast sums expended in these services far exceed the requirements of national safety, and are the outward and visible signs of a body of policy. They contribute nothing to restoration and add nothing to our wealth or to our capacity to produce it. The British Empire has been built up by careful and just administration and by the personal initiative and industry of its people, and not by a prodigal expenditure of this kind in distant places upon a handful of people.

These things, with many more like them that could be cited, betoken a spirit of adventure and of a system of rule that is based on force and not on securing the consent

---

* First Report, p. 57.

of the governed that is altogether foreign to the statecraft that has built up the British Empire. No better example could be afforded than that of the expenditure in Egypt for which the estimates for the present year are but little less than those of the one just closed. The excess in these charges arises out of ignoring the principles recommended by Lord Milner and the substitution for them of a policy of repression. This, again, appears for the present to have been partially abandoned, but the distrust that it gave rise to is represented in the expenditure now being incurred.

In the same way, the disposition which has characterised the substitution of the Supreme Council and other conferences for the discharge of many duties for which the machinery of the League of Nations was set up to deal, are manifestations of an autocratic method altogether inimical to the abatement of international rivalries. These conferences have achieved very little, and at a great cost, whilst, on the contrary, the League of Nations, whenever they have had responsibilities put upon them—as in the matters of the Aaland Islands, Albania and the

Polish frontiers—have achieved much more valuable results by less ostentatious methods.

The present policy appears to commit us to a system of grouping of the Powers that past experience has shown to be ineffective for the maintenance of peace, and that leads to War Service expenditures that are beyond our present means, and that arrest the processes of real restoration.

First things should come first. And the first thing surely to make up for the losses of the war is to devote our thoughts and powers to improving the capacity and efficiency of our own people.

If we compare the gigantic sums which have just been criticised with the proposed grant of £200,000 for the restoration or re-placement of insanitary houses throughout Great Britain, the latter appears to be a very mean figure. But it relates to something that as a cause of physical incapacity, of moral evil and of social unrest, is of vastly greater consequences to the British Empire than the occupation, say, of the Mosul district which costs far more, or even of the whole of Mesopotamia. It would be possible by the devotion of only a small fraction of the savings that would follow a change in the disposition of our policy to provide a scheme of restoration and of replacement of insanitary houses that would be adequate, if sustained, and at the same time commensurate with the capacities of the industries concerned.

No one has yet told us in any authoritative and reliable way what the potential advantages of Mesopotamia really are, and no responsible soldier defends the expenditure of £120,000,000 on that country during the past three years on the grounds of imperial strategic necessity. But the interest and sinking fund charges on the debt incurred by this costly occupation would almost suffice, as an annual contribution in aid, to redeem the slums of this country. The advantages accruing to the people from the two forms of expenditure are not to be compared with one another.

In order, however, to justify that comparison it is necessary to provide the outline of a possible scheme of national assistance of slum restoration with an estimate of its cost.

We once had a Naval Defence Act covering a period of construction for a series of years, and a similar project, with sufficient margins for annual adjustments, according to the state of trade, is necessary and is feasible for the replacement or reconstruction of insanitary dwellings.

It would be necessary to limit the charges falling upon the State and to provide incentives to ingenuity and economy for those entrusted with the work, and in that connection we must learn what lessons we can from the experiences of the past three years.

One of these lessons is that unless the country is to be needlessly exploited there must be a more effective check on the high costs of building. It is true that the alternative demands on the building trade during the years 1919 and 1920 were as unprecedented as they were extravagant, and are not likely to recur to the same extent, but an intimate knowledge of what happened during that time leads to the conclusion that neither the associations of the master builders nor the trade unions concerned, as they exist to-day, can be relied upon to check extravagant costs.

In any future scheme, covering a long period of effort, the community should be equipped with more effective powers. They would perhaps rarely require to be exercised because the fact that they existed would often suffice, as has been the case in other instances.

To this end at various times during the recent housing effort proposals were submitted to the Cabinet that were based to some extent upon what we had found to be effective at the Ministry of Munitions in securing a limitation of costs. The proposals were not accepted.

Measures of that kind, however, will probably be required, and they could be adopted without damage to industry.

Somewhat later on in the efforts to obtain houses at less extravagant prices the building guilds came into existence. They were at first necessarily handicapped by a lack of skilled technical advice and assistance, and the occasion of their commencement presented other difficulties. Nevertheless, progress was made, and they afforded an illustration of co-operative effort that was of a most promising kind.

Another desirable condition of State assistance should be that its contribution should be made on such a basis that it entailed within itself an incentive to economical working. It is not now possible to go back to the scheme submitted in 1917 in pursuance of the recommendations of Lord Salisbury's committee, nor are those proposals specially applicable to the question of slum improvement. Nevertheless, the cost of the work done, subject to a proper limitation, should be a governing consideration, and the free acceptance of all charges beyond the yield of a penny rate clearly does not contain either a sufficient incentive to economy, or a reasonable limitation on the liabilities of the State.

The houses that were acquired and reconstructed in London during the times of high prices prevailing in 1919 and 1920 provided family tenements at a cost of some £720 apiece. At that time interest and sinking fund charges were 6½ per cent. per annum on the money borrowed. At present the equivalent charges are not more than 5½ per cent., and the cost of building has greatly fallen.

Acquisitions and reconstructions on similar lines at the present time would probably not involve an expenditure of more than £450 per dwelling provided. At present day money rates, after deducting the rents obtainable and making a fair allowance for repairs and other charges, the annual loss per annum on such a house would probably not exceed £10.

In any scheme of this kind, however, allowance would have to be made for the fact that a large number of the houses are worthless, and would require to be demolished and replaced by satisfactory dwellings either on the site itself or elsewhere.

To set against this, many small houses would be needed for elderly couples, unmarried persons and others who would not wish to have so much accommodation as is provided for a family. In so far also as a sensible foresight would suggest, certain portions of the sites acquired could, consistently with a proper rehousing scheme, be made use of for commercial or industrial purposes, and the charges falling on the housing account would be accordingly diminished.

Under the arrangements made during 1919 and 1920, Local Authorities are already in possession of land sufficient to provide sites for 400,000 houses, so that, so far as rehousing was not undertaken on the sites taken for improvement schemes, a great deal of land is already available, and the cost of it has been included in the cost of the house-building schemes that have been arrested. This land represents a very substantial contribution by the State to any houses erected thereon, and so far as it was used for new accommodation that was a necessary ingredient of an improvement scheme, the value of the State's contribution in respect of it should be accounted for in estimating the exchequer contribution. If we bear all these considerations in mind, even at the present costs of building, the necessities of the case would appear to be fully met if we allow that the annual loss per dwelling acquired, and either reconstructed or replaced, should not exceed £15. The State's contribution to the loss could take various forms, but it might fairly be limited to a minimum of two-thirds, with an allowance up to four-fifths in poor districts. If the liability in respect of all schemes represented the maximum loss permitted—which, of course, would not be the case—the contributions of the State per dwelling would vary from ten to twelve pounds per annum, the latter figure being the maximum. The proportion of the loss left to fall upon the locality would provide a real incentive to economy as well as a fair share of the burden.

A programme on these lines, which provided for the reconstruction or replacement in town and country of 500,000 insanitary or insufficient homes, would occupy a number of years, and would represent at the end of that time an annual State contribution of from five to six million pounds. A scheme of that kind would not by any means meet all the need, but it would provide a very substantial contribution thereto, and would be of sufficient magnitude to occupy time enough for different expedients to be tested and for the development of a more efficient future policy.

It need not exclude the encouragement of new building by private enterprise. Indeed, a number of inducements could be offered with that object in view. The methods of rating and the basis of assessment of values offer a number of opportunities for providing such assistance and encouragement, but they have purposely been omitted. If, however, we are to assume that the present basis will remain for a considerable time, there do not seem to be sufficient grounds for rejecting the proposal that new houses, built within, say, the next ten years, should pay only half-rates for a period, say, of twenty years after completion. It would stimulate building, and would not be unfair to other ratepayers, since in any case the new or reconstructed houses, even at half-rates, would represent a substantial addition to the rateable value of a district.

It is not to be expected that, after having spent some years in the Department of State that is specially concerned with these matters, one should be unaware of the objections which may be raised against such proposals, but they are not made without a careful examination of different alternatives, and it would be cowardly and unpatriotic to avoid making constructive suggestions.

What, by comparison, is the cost of neglect? It is that we should be committed to a continuing, and even to an increasing, expenditure upon combating the results of these deplorable housing conditions; for public opinion would demand and no Government would refuse to spend money upon the treatment of the sickness and ill-health, as well as upon the unemployment that such conditions produce. Beyond this there would remain a source of moral damage, of social and industrial unrest that would inflict incalculable loss. Contented people are easy to govern for they are prepared to govern and control themselves. A wretched home does not allow of contentment. The costliness of popular discontent even in a single year might well exceed the total charge which such an undertaking as has been proposed would involve.

There is no direction in which the thrift, the contentment and the physical and intellectual capacity of our people can be more directly or plainly promoted than in this. It may be drab and unattractive in its detail, but in its nature and in its fulfilment, it is heroic. It is worthy of sacrifice and of all the powers of discipline and statesmanship that we possess. We should, moreover, throughout the years of work be conscious that the pledged word of the British people to the living as well as to the dead remained unbroken.

Lightning Source UK Ltd.
Milton Keynes UK
UKHW050022140121
376872UK00024B/510